Music Minus One Vocals

Lush and Lovely Standards
with Orchestra

songs in the style of
BARBRA STREISAND

T0056480

2190

Acting would have to wait a bit but her voice could not be denied for long. After developing a nightclub act that she debuted in 1960 at a Greenwich Village club, she dropped one of the letters from her first name, becoming Barbra Streisand. She worked at several New York nightclubs including the Bon Soir and the Blue Angel as she built up her repertoire and the power of her voice. She made her debut on The Tonight Show in 1961 when Orson Bean substituted for the host Jack Paar, singing Harold Arlen's "A Sleepin' Bee." In 1962 Streisand made her first appearance on Broadway in a small role in the musical I Can Get It For You Wholesale. She also held her own with Judy Garland on television, earning Garland's praise.

With the release of her first record The Barbra Streisand Album in 1963 (which won two Grammy Awards), the singer was on her way to the top. Success followed upon success from then on. She starred as entertainer Fanny Brice in the show Funny Girl. Among the songs that she sang in the play (and eventually the movie of the same name) were "People," "Don't Rain On My Parade" and the Fanny Brice hit "My Man." Each of her records (which include The Second Barbra Streisand Album, The Third Album and My Name Is Barbra) were best sellers, featuring vintage material such as "Happy Days Are Here Again" along with newer Broadway songs such as ".Somewhere" and "He Touched Me." In addition, Streisand had success with her four television specials during 1965-67.

During this period, Barbra Streisand realized her goal to become a top actress. She debuted in Hollywood in 1968 with Funny Girl, sharing the 1968 Academy Award for Best Actress with Katharine Hepburn. Hello Dolly and On A Clear Day You Can See Forever were popular musicals. She revealed her skill at comedy in 1972's What's Up Doc and melted many people's hearts with her performance in the following year's The Way We Were which included her singing of the movie's theme song. 1976's A Star Is Born yielded her hit "Evergreen." Of her later films, Yentl from 1983 meant a great deal to Streisand, who wrote the script in addition to starring.

Streisand sang more modern material in the 1970's than she had previously and, despite the dominance of rock, she had hits with "The Way We Were," "Evergreen," "No More Tears," "You Don't Bring Me Flowers" and "The Main Event." Her version of "Tomorrow" from 1978 was also popular as were her early 1980's pop recordings "Memory" and "Woman In Love."

Since that time, Barbra Streisand has retained her fame while having a dual career as a singer and an actress. 1985's The Broadway Album found her returning to some of the vintage songs that she sang earlier in her career along with some newer Broadway tunes. Concentrating on directing films and becoming involved in political affairs, she was less active as a singer for a few years until recording 1993's Back To Broadway, a CD that debuted at #1 on the pop charts.

Despite her talents, Streisand has always suffered a bit from stage fright, making her public appearances as a singer rare. In 1994 when she had a tour of the United States, all of the tickets sold out in less than an hour. Clearly her popularity had not faded and, even 20 years later, she can still fill stadiums whenever she decides to perform.

Her hit records of the past 20 years include 1996's "I Finally Found Someone," "If You Ever Leave Me," 2003's The Movie Album and 2007's Love Is The Answer. The biggest selling female singer of all time, Barbra Streisand is the only artist to have #1 albums in five different decades. In addition, she is one of only 15 performers to have won an Oscar, an Emmy (she has five), a Tony and Grammy awards; she has eight of the latter.

She has had quite a career and at 72, Barbra Streisand is not done yet.

Scott Yanow,
author of 11 books including The Jazz Singers,
The Great Jazz Guitarists, Swing, Jazz On Film
and Jazz On Record 1917-76

Lush and Lovely Standards with Orchestra

songs in the style of BARBRA STREISAND

CONTENTS

ISBN 978-1-941566-88-6

MMO 2190

I Concentrate On You
from "Broadway Melody Of 1940"

Words and Music by Cole Porter

6

I've Got A Crush On You
from "Strike Up The Band"

Music and Lyrics by
George Gershwin and Ira Gershwin

8

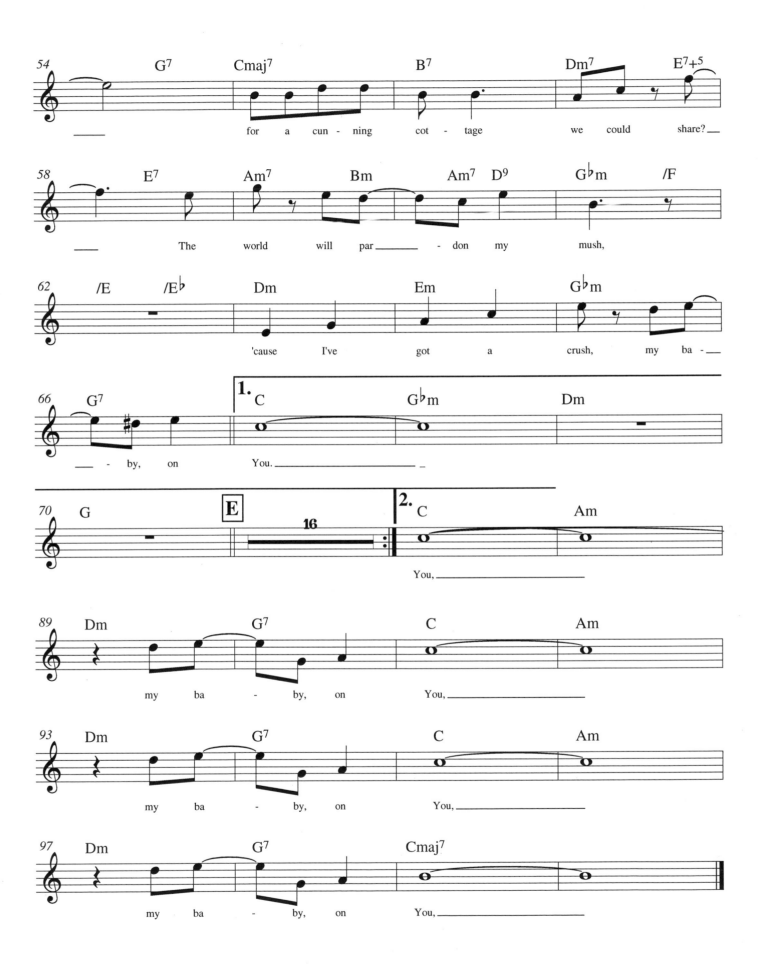

I Remember You
from the Paramount Picture "The Fleets In"

Words by Johnny Mercer
Music by Victor Schertzinger

Softly, As I Leave You

Music by Antonio DeVita
English Lyric by Hal Shaper

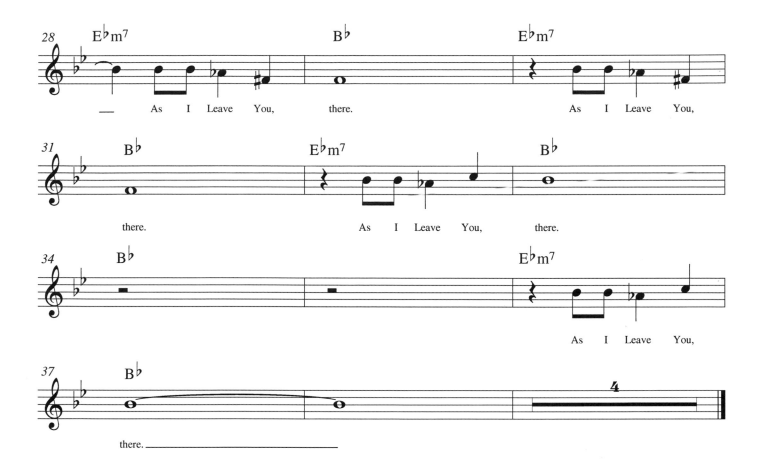

Almost Like Being In Love

from "Brigadoon"

Lyrics by Alan Jay Lerner
Music by Frederick Loewe

I'm Glad There Is You
(In This World Of Ordinary People)

Words and Music by
Paul Madeira and Jimmy Dorsey

When I Fall In Love

from "One Minute To Zero"

Words by Edward Heyman
Music by Victor Young

Dream A Little Dream Of Me

Words by Gus Kahn
Music by Wilbur Schwandt and Fabian Andree

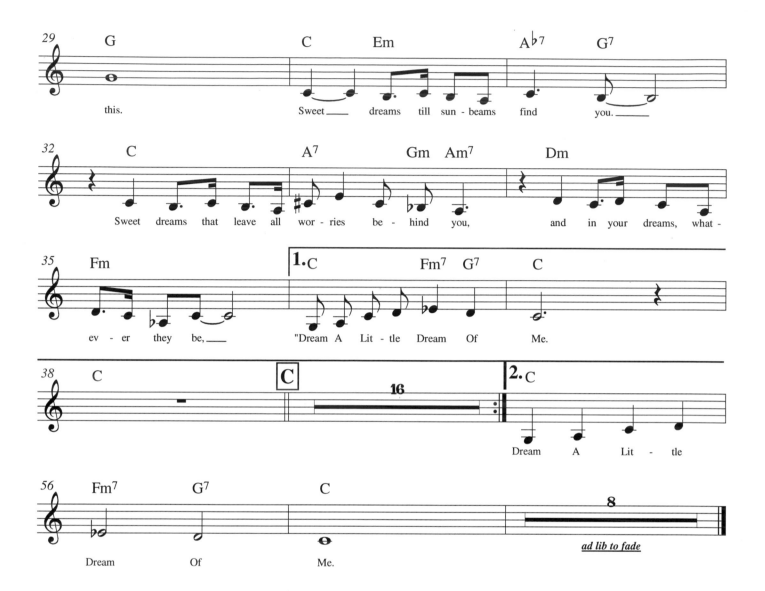

Ev'ry Time We Say Goodbye

from "Seven Lively Arts"

Words and Music by Cole Porter

Music Minus One
50 Executive Boulevard • Elmsford, New York 10523-1325
914-592-1188 • e-mail: info@musicminusone.com
www.musicminusone.com

MMO 2190

ISBN 978-1-941566-88-6